# A LITTLE BOOK OF TOBACCO

**A Little Book of Alcohol**
**Activities to Explore Alcohol Issues with Young People**
**2nd edition**
ISBN 978 1 84905 303 7
eISBN 978 0 85700 628 8

**A Little Book of Drugs**
**Activities to Explore Drugs Issues with Young People**
**2nd edition**
ISBN 978 1 84905 304 4
eISBN 978 0 85700 629 5

**Games and Activities for Exploring Feelings with Children**
**Giving Children the Confidence to Navigate Emotions and Friendships**
ISBN 978 1 84905 222 1
eISBN 978 0 85700 459 8

**101 Things to Do on the Street**
**Games and Resources for Detached, Outreach and Street-Based Youth Work**
**2nd edition**
ISBN 978 1 84905 187 3
eISBN 978 0 85700 419 2

**Let's Talk Relationships**
**Activities for Exploring Love, Sex, Friendship and Family with Young People**
**2nd edition**
ISBN 978 1 84905 136
eISBN 978 0 85700 340 9

**Cyberbullying**
**Activities to Help Children and Teens to Stay Safe in a Texting, Twittering, Social Networking World**
ISBN 978 1 84905 105 7
eISBN 978 0 85700 228 0

**Working with Young Men**
**Activities for Exploring Personal, Social and Emotional Issues**
**2nd edition**
ISBN 978 1 84905 101 9
eISBN 978 0 85700 282 2

**Working with Young Women**
**Activities for Exploring Personal, Social and Emotional Issues**
**2nd edition**
ISBN 978 1 84905 095 1
eISBN 978 0 85700 372 0

# A LITTLE BOOK OF TOBACCO

## ACTIVITIES TO EXPLORE SMOKING ISSUES WITH YOUNG PEOPLE

Vanessa Rogers

Jessica Kingsley *Publishers*
London and Philadelphia

First published in 2012
by Jessica Kingsley Publishers
116 Pentonville Road
London N1 9JB, UK
and
400 Market Street, Suite 400
Philadelphia, PA 19106, USA

*www.jkp.com*

**Library of Congress Cataloging in Publication Data**
Rogers, Vanessa.
  A little book of tobacco : activities to explore smoking issues with young people / Vanessa Rogers.
    p. cm.
  ISBN 978-1-84905-305-1 (alk. paper)
  1. Smoking. 2. Teenagers--Tobacco use. I. Title.
  HV5740.R64 2012
  362.29'6--dc23
                              2012025298


**British Library Cataloguing in Publication Data**
A CIP catalogue record for this book is available from the British Library

ISBN 978 1 84905 305 1
eISBN 978 0 85700 630 1


Printed and bound in Great Britain

# CONTENTS

# ACKNOWLEDGEMENTS

I would like to thank:

Dave Price (A-DASH), Donna Lancaster (Youth Worker), Jonathan Jack (Hertfordshire Youth Connexions), Gillian Porter (QE11), Deborah Mulroney (HCC School Improvement and Development Service), Joshua Oakes-Rogers (Simon Balle School), Darren Godfrey (Essex Youth Service), Geoff Fisher (Peterborough Youth Service), Ann McKay (Youth Worker).

Thanks also to any other youth workers who have been a part of the projects mentioned.

# ABOUT THE AUTHOR

Vanessa Rogers is a qualified teacher and youth worker with a master's degree in Community Education. She has over ten years' experience within the Hertfordshire Youth Service both at practitioner and management levels. Prior to achieving national recognition for her work Vanessa managed a wide range of services for young people, including a large youth centre and targeted detached projects for Hertfordshire County Council. She now devises and delivers professional development training and writes for *Children & Young People Now*. In addition she has been commissioned to devise training packs for a wide range of organizations, including the BBC.

This book is one of 21 practical resources written by Vanessa to support the development of creative youth work and social education.

Her website www.vanessarogers.co.uk gives detailed information about further titles, training and consultancy visits.

# INTRODUCTION

Deciding whether to smoke, or not, is a personal decision that most people will make at some point when growing up. This resource is a diverse collection of activities developed to help inform that decision. Aimed at those working with young people aged 13–19 (up to 24 with additional needs), the activities and games give information, explore values and help build skills, promoting healthy choices.

It is important to remember that although young people are likely to have come into contact with cigarettes and may even have made decisions around whether to smoke or not, that doesn't mean that they are fully aware of the legal, health and social impacts of their decision. It is also the opportunity to reinforce that it is possible to give up successfully and to signpost individuals to local organizations that can support this decision.

The book is divided into sections, as described below. Each of the activities in the sections can be used as a 'stand-alone' activity or put together with others to build a comprehensive curriculum over a few weeks.

## Warm-ups

This section offers short activities and exercises to open a session around tobacco or to re-energize a group after a discussion. Easy to use, these are ideas to introduce issues and enable you to begin to assess the level of knowledge and attitudes to smoking within the group.

## Making decisions about smoking

This section offers ideas to explore cigarette and tobacco smoking and looks at the role other people play in the decision to smoke or not. There are activities to explore values and attitudes to smoking, and opportunities to explore issues such as the legalities, taxation on tobacco and the financial implications.

It also contains activities to consider the barriers to giving up and includes quit tips and some ideas for action planning and finding the support to make giving up smoking successful.

## Health

Including ideas for group and individual work, the activities in this section look at four main areas:

- Factual information and health education about tobacco.

- The exploration of attitudes and values, including peer influence and reducing risk.

- Opportunities to develop the skills to make healthy choices.

- Quitting smoking and finding support to stop.

## Marketing and the role of the media

In this section the activities focus on the role of advertising companies and the methods they use to promote and market cigarettes and smoking. It explores values and attitudes around smoking and encourages young people to see the marketing ploys used through a range of media to target a new audience, namely young people, and judge for themselves the integrity of the methods used.

From the glitz of Hollywood and the multi-billion dollar movie industry to the pubs of Northern England featured in Soapland, characters are shown smoking. Onscreen images may glamorize, normalize and incentivize smoking, particularly among young people. These activities challenge the appropriateness of this by considering the messages given and looking at some of the more positive role models for young people.

## The global perspective

Although the number of smokers quitting is increasing in high income regions of the world, for example the USA and UK, Cancer Research UK has highlighted growing concerns from governments that the numbers of smokers are actually increasing in places such as Malawi, Zimbabwe and other low and middle income countries.

There is growing evidence to suggest that this discrepancy in trends is due to differing legislation regulating advertising, promotion and sponsorship as well as less awareness of the health risks. Alongside this are concerns about the exploitation of tobacco farmers and the continued practice of child labour, particularly in Africa.

This section aims to raise awareness with young people about these concerns and encourages them to take a global perspective on the issue.

## Review tips

The final pages suggest a few ideas for reviewing and reinforcing learning. It is important to allow time at the end of a session for these as they help evaluate the effectiveness of sessions and inform your needs analysis for further work.

# GROUND RULES

Make it clear before you start that you have made no assumptions about the number of young people who either smoke or who have experimented with tobacco in some form. Some young people may be open about their habit, whilst others are eager to hide what they do. For both non-smokers and smokers it is important that they make choices based on knowledge and understanding, which is the aim of the activities in this book.

It is important that facilitators consider that young people may have close relatives who are suffering from smoking-related illnesses and that this topic could provoke some distress. A strategy for support should be agreed before the session, which can be put into place if appropriate.

Find out what support is available for any smokers wishing to quit and use some of the sessions that explore the difficulties in giving up and strategies to resist the temptation to smoke again.

To ensure a safe learning environment it is good practice to negotiate ground rules with the young people at the start, outlining confidentiality and the limits to it. Refer back to them as the sessions progress so they provide a familiar framework for working safely and respectfully together.

Equally, as the issues around smoking can be extremely sensitive make sure that confidentiality and the need to respect each others' points of view are fully considered.

# TOBACCO INFORMATION

Tobacco consumption is responsible for killing around 5.4 million smokers worldwide every year. This is more than the total number of people who live in the whole of the West Midlands and Greater Manchester, or almost all of the people who live in Los Angeles and Chicago.

In the UK alone more than 100,000 people die per year from tobacco-related deaths. That's equivalent to losing the entire population of the Isle of Wight.

## Basic health information

As well as seriously damaging your finances, smoking can also cause major health problems both in the short and long term. As a rough guide here are the main areas for concern:

1.  Bad skin. Smoking restricts blood vessels, preventing oxygen and nutrients from getting to the skin, which can cause premature wrinkles and ageing of the skin.

2.  Bad breath and/or yellow teeth.

3.  Smelly clothes and hair. The smell of stale smoke lingers and is hard to remove.

4.  Reduced athletic performance. Smoking can increase heartbeat, decrease circulation and lead to shortness of breath.

5.  Increased risk of injury and slower healing time. Smoking affects the body's ability to produce collagen – so common sports injuries such as damaged tendons and ligaments heal more slowly.

6. Reduced immunity to common illness. Smokers tend to get more colds, flu, bronchitis and pneumonia than non-smokers.

7. Throat, lung, stomach and bladder cancer.

8. Higher risk of osteoporosis and decreased bone density.

9. Fertility problems and erectile dysfunction.

10. Higher risk of emphysema (lung disease), heart disease and stroke.

## Short history of tobacco

Tobacco and smoking has a long history. Experts believe that tobacco began growing about 8000 years ago and people have been using it to smoke or chew in different forms since then.

The tobacco plant is believed to have been widely available in America since the first century AD. Evidence of smoking in the form of pictures dates back to the 11th century.

The native people of the Americas considered tobacco a gift from the Great Spirit, and they used it in their religious practices.

An early explorer of the Americas, Rodrigo de Jerez, brought the habit of smoking tobacco back to Spain around 1504. By 1511, smoking was popular throughout Spain, and by 1531 Europeans were cultivating tobacco, the 'sweet' *Nicotiana tabacum*, in Santo Domingo.

It is estimated that the 20th century brought about a change in the number of smokers and, more importantly, the number of illnesses caused by this habit. When cigarettes first started being manufactured, they were rolled by hand and it is said that a skilled individual could roll up to four cigarettes every minute, which meant about 2000 cigarettes a day.

Afterwards machines designed for making cigarettes were invented and the production was suddenly boosted, so people could buy and smoke them more easily.

Despite more knowledge being available about the harm smoking does to the human body, worldwide the number of smokers has increased year on year. Arguably, these numbers are likely to keep increasing unless everyone takes an attitude to start being more responsible for their own health. Despite changes to laws and attempts by successive governments and health organizations to inform people of the dangers, particularly targeting young people not to start the habit, there are still estimated to be 1.5 billion smokers worldwide.

## UK smoking information

Since 1 October 2007 it is against the law to sell tobacco to anyone under the age of 18. The law includes sale of cigarettes, cigars and tobacco for roll-your-own and pipes and also rolling papers. If a young person is over the age of 18, but looks under 21, they can be asked for picture ID to prove it. Anyone selling tobacco to an underage person could face a heavy fine.

On 1 July 2007, England introduced a new law to make virtually all enclosed public places and workplaces in England smoke-free.

The Tobacco Advertising and Promotion Act 2002 prohibits the advertising and promotion of tobacco products in England, Scotland, Wales and Northern Ireland, including sponsorship.

Tobacco products must carry the general warning 'Tobacco seriously damages health', and cigarette packets must carry a second warning on the back of the pack selected from a list of 15, such as 'Smoking when pregnant harms your baby' and 'Protect children: don't make them breathe your smoke.'

In 2012 the Welsh Assembly placed a ban on smoking on hospital sites in Wales, and is currently considering implementing a smoking ban for smokers in cars too.

## American smoking information

From the American Cancer Society:

- Eighty-nine per cent of people who ever try a cigarette try by age 18. Almost no one starts the smoking habit during adulthood.

- Seventy per cent of adolescent smokers say they would never have started if they could choose again. That's because the nicotine in cigarettes is addictive. The risk of becoming addicted to nicotine is between one in two and one in three.

- Tobacco is responsible for nearly one in every five deaths in the United States. It is the largest cause of preventable death.

- More than 400,000 people die every year from smoking-related diseases. That's more than from alcohol, crack, heroin, murder, suicide, car accidents and AIDS combined!

## Australia smoking information

From ASH Australia:

- In Australia, a child under 14 dies from tobacco every ten days.

- Around 110,000 Australian schoolchildren smoke regularly – and many more are exposed to tobacco smoke in homes, cars and public places.

- Most smokers start before turning 18 – the average Australian smoking initiation age is just under 16.

- In Tasmania from 1 March 2012, new laws make all outdoor dining areas smoke free, as well as sports and patrolled swim areas, bus shelters and playgrounds. Other states are following.

- From 1 January 2012, tobacco display is not permitted in any general retail outlet in Australia.

- By December 2012, Australia's tobacco plain packaging law will take effect.

## Canada smoking information

There are two federal acts that address tobacco products and their use at federal level in Canada:[1]

1. The Tobacco Act administered by Health Canada governs the manufacture, sale, labelling and promotion of tobacco products and provides the authority to the Governor in Council to make regulations on these issues.

   The Tobacco Act prohibits the sale of tobacco products to young persons (18 years of age or less) and requires retailers of tobacco products to post signs that inform the public that furnishing tobacco products to young persons is prohibited by law.

2. The Non-Smokers Health Act, which restricts smoking in federally regulated workplaces and public places under federal jurisdiction and provides the Governor in Council with the authority to make regulations on these issues.

---

[1] For more information and details about these, go to www.hc-sc.gc.ca.

## Smoking and the media

Studies suggest that smoking in movies misleads young people into thinking that tobacco use is normal, acceptable, socially beneficial and more common than it really is. The current rate of smoking scenes in Hollywood films has returned to the high levels of the 1950s, after reaching its lowest levels in 1980.

## Global information[2]

Government-owned China National Tobacco is the world's largest producer of tobacco and accounts for one-third of the global market. Other producers (in order of production) are Brazil, India, United States, Malawi, Indonesia and then the rest of the world. British American Tobacco (BAT) is the world's second biggest cigarette company.

The Framework Convention on Tobacco Control (FCTC) is the first global public health treaty developed in response to the increasing tobacco epidemic and covers a wide range of issues to reduce the global harm caused by tobacco, including aggressive advertising. It came into force on 27 February, 2005, and by 2009 had been signed by 168 of the 192 WHO member states, making it one of the most widely embraced treaties in UN history.

---

2   www.dh.gov.uk; www.bbc.co.uk; http://tobaccocontrol.bmj.com; www.statistics.gov.uk.

## Quitting

It is important to consider that some young people may already be regular smokers. This does not mean that they will all be ready to give up, but after raising awareness of some of the issues around smoking it is important to have details of local support organizations.

Remind smokers that just because they have tried to give up and failed, it does not mean that they won't succeed next time. For details of how to develop a quit plan or more information abut nicotine addiction, go to www.smokefree.nhs.uk.

# WARM-UPS

# SMOKING AND FITNESS

## Aim

This quick warm-up simulates how heavy smoking can affect breathing and the ability to exercise.

## You will need

- A straw for each person
- Stopwatch or mobile phone with a stopwatch function

## How to do it

Start the warm-up by asking the young people about the sports they play and the enjoyment they get out of exercise.

Set everyone the following timed tasks:

1. March on the spot for one minute.

2. Jog on the spot for one minute.

3. Run on the spot for one minute.

4. Do star jumps for one minute.

Congratulate everyone after each round and then give a straw to each person. This time explain that when you shout 'Go!' everyone should place their straw in their mouth and plug their nose before attempting to run on the spot for a further minute. This will simulate how a heavy smoker or person with emphysema breathes and the difficulties they might encounter whilst trying to exercise.

Call time and review their experiences.

# TOBACCO CROSSWORD

## Aim

This is a simple crossword puzzle to assess young people's knowledge about tobacco and smoking.

## You will need

- A crossword puzzle and clues per three young people (ideally enlarged onto A3 size paper to make it easier for the group to work on)
- Pens

## How to do it

Most young people will have some experience of crossword puzzles, so this should need little explanation.

Divide the young people into groups of three and give each group a copy of the crossword and a pen. Allow enough time for each group to discuss and write their answers into the boxes, using the clues to help them.

When the crosswords are complete go through the answers together, inviting the young people to check out anything they have not heard of before or didn't understand.

The group with the most correct answers wins the game and can set one more clue for another word relating to the topic of tobacco and smoking for the rest of the young people to answer.

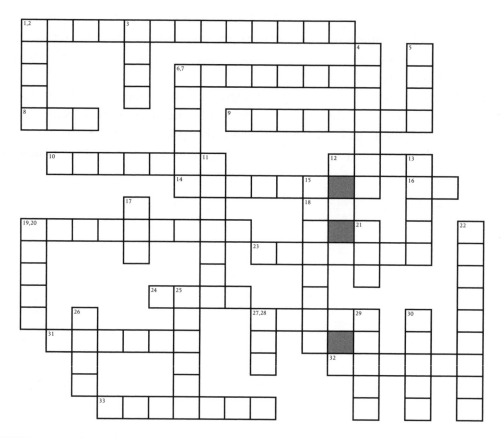

## Tobacco crossword clues

The clues to this crossword reveal words that relate to the topic of tobacco and smoking.

### Across

1. Each packet comes with one of these on it (6, 7)
6. Another word for an anti-smoking crusade
8. Low – – – cigarettes can give smokers an excuse not to quit
9. Quitting smoking will improve your chances of having a healthy baby if you are this
10. People use this instead of a match
12. Smokers inhale smoke – – – – into their lungs
14. Heavy smoking can make your teeth look like this
16. If you have given up you become an – – smoker
18. To buy cigarettes, you are often asked for this as proof of age
19. There are more than 4000 of these in a single cigarette
23. A collective term for people who smoke
24. One benefit of not smoking is having more of this to spend on other things

27. This is a common place for smokers to get cancer

31. If someone is smoking nearby you inhale – – – – – hand smoke

32. Some people worry they will put this on if they give up smoking

33. The best place to put out a lit cigarette

## Down

2. Smoking can cause disease of this major organ

3. Smoking can cause long- and short- – – – – damage to the human body

4. Another way of saying 'breathed in'

5. To give up

7. Smoking is the leading preventable cause of this disease

11. Hand-rolled cigarettes

13. Another word for 'friends'

15. Unscramble the letters CNNEITIO

17. People who smoke are likely to do this younger

20. What a smoker does to try to get some tar and mucus out of their lungs

21. Cigarettes come in packs of this and 20

22. A white stick, wrapped in paper, that is smoked

25. A term to describe someone hooked on something

26. Part of a tobacco plant

28. The opposite of high tar

29. Smoking can make your clothes, breath and hair do this

30. Smoked like a cigarette

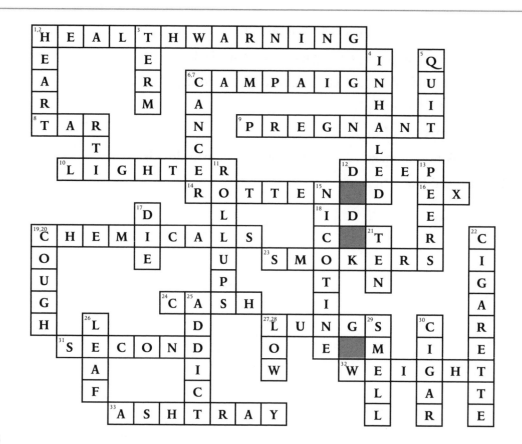

# SMOKING – THE FACTS QUIZ

## Aim

This quiz is a quick icebreaker to check out young people's existing knowledge around smoking and the tobacco industry. It introduces the topic, promotes discussion and highlights areas that need additional learning opportunities.

## You will need

- Pens
- Copies of the quiz sheet

## How to do it

Hand out pens and a copy of the quiz, asking the young people to tick whether they think the statements contained are 'True' or 'False'. Ask them to work individually to start with, stressing that if they don't know the answer it is OK to have a guess.

Once everyone has completed the quiz, form a circle or gather the group together so you can go through the questions asking participants to suggest answers and taking time to discuss any points raised or answer any questions.

Once the quiz is complete, ask the group to count up their scores. How much did they know? Which statement did most get wrong?

## Smoking – the facts quiz

| | | TRUE | FALSE |
|---|---|---|---|
| 1. | Yesterday, smoking tobacco will have killed 180 people in the UK | | |
| 2. | Worldwide over 15 billion cigarettes are smoked every day | | |
| 3. | British American Tobacco made 1.6 billion pounds (about 2.5 billion US dollars) of profit in 2006 | | |
| 4. | Currently in the UK young women are more likely to smoke regularly than young men | | |
| 5. | Kenya is one of the heaviest smoking countries in the world | | |
| 6. | In Malawi, in Africa, they have banned child labour on tobacco farms as it is against the worldwide UN Convention on the Rights of the Child | | |
| 7. | Smokers inhale over 2000 chemicals from a cigarette | | |

✓

| | | TRUE | FALSE |
|---|---|---|---|
| 8. | In Germany they have electronically locked cigarette vending machines, and you have to have ID to prove you are over 16 to use them | | |
| 9. | The children of smokers are twice as likely to become a smoker as they grow older | | |
| 10. | Ex-smokers live longer than people who keep smoking | | |

## Quiz answers

1. False. Three hundred people in the UK die each day from smoking.

2. True.

3. False. They are the world's second biggest cigarette company and made 2.6 billion pounds (over 4 billion dollars) of profits in 2006.

4. True. According to the NHS survey Drug Use, Smoking and Drinking Among Young People in England 2007.

5. True. According to the Kenyan Ministry of Health up to 15 per cent of under-15-year-olds now smoke and approximately 45 per cent of 18- to 30-year-olds.

6. False. Malawi has the highest incidence of child labour on tobacco farms in Sub-Saharan Africa.

7. False. Smokers inhale over 4000 chemicals from a cigarette, out of which 400 are poisonous toxins, including carbon monoxide.

8. True. In 2007 electronic locking devices based on proof-of-age (via electronic cash cards or a European driving licence) were installed in approximately 500,000 vending machines across Germany to restrict the purchase of cigarettes to those over the age of 16.

9. False. According to the UK NHS the children of smokers are three times more likely to smoke.

10. True. Statistically those that give up smoking have increased health benefits over time.

*Sources:* ASH – *You've got to be kidding report, BAT's African Footprint* (www.ash.org.uk); Cancer Research UK – Policy Statement on the Tobacco Industry (www.cancerresearchuk.org); Tobacco Control – Implementation of electronic locking devices for adolescents at German tobacco vending machines: Intended and unintended changes of supply and demand (http://tobaccocontrol.bmj.com); NHS – *Smoking, Drinking and Drug Use among Young People in England in 2010 report* (www.ic.nhs.uk).

# THE ART OF SHOPPING

## Aim

This activity encourages young people to think about the influences that affect their shopping and lifestyle choices.

## You will need

- A4 paper and pens

## How to do it

Ask each young person to write down at the top of an A4 sheet the last thing they bought that cost £20 ($30) or more and then fold the paper down to cover it. Then ask how they found out about the item. For example, was it recommended? Did they see it in a magazine or was it an impulse buy? They should write this down and fold the paper concertina-style again.

Now ask them to think about the thought process they went through before deciding to buy. For example, if it was an item of clothing how did they decide what to wear? Point out that people rarely, if ever, go into a shop and just buy the first thing they see that fits! Most people choose clothes that reflect the image they want to present to the world. If it was an electrical item, for example an MP3 player, how did they decide which brand to purchase? Was it price alone, or style or functionality? Allow time for them to write down as many ideas as possible.

Next ask them to write down where they bought it from, for example, a brand name shop, internet store or bidding site such as eBay, once again folding down their answer. Finally ask them to write down why they decided to buy it from that particular place. For example, was it based on the cost, the store itself, availability, or perhaps it was an ethical choice based on the values of the seller.

Divide the main group into fours/fives and ask them to go through their papers together, opening and discussing each point one by one. Ask them to note down any key themes emerging.

Invite feedback from each group, asking further questions and pulling out similarities. Go on to explain that companies spend millions of pounds or dollars employing marketers who try to understand why people buy what they buy. Once they work this out they then promote the product to the people they think are most likely to buy it; for example, holding competitions, designing packaging, adverts, posters, and even endorsements by famous people. In this way promotion is a part of our daily lives. The clothes we choose to wear and the food we choose to eat are almost entirely the result of promotion. Conclude by suggesting that the tobacco industry is no different, although regulations have severely limited its choice of promotional tools.

# ODD ONE OUT

## Aim

This quick warm-up raises awareness of the chemicals that are in each cigarette smoked.

## You will need

- Copies of the 'Odd One Out' cards

## How to do it

Divide the young people into small groups and give each group a set of cards. Explain that this is essentially a sorting game.

Start by saying that there is far more in a cigarette than just tobacco and paper. Many chemicals are used that are found in lots of common household products too. Ask the young people to look through the cards and take out the ones with the name of something that they think does NOT contain a chemical also found in a cigarette.

Allow time for discussion and decisions to be made and then call time. Go through the list of substances asking which ones each group thought did not contain any chemicals also found in a cigarette.

Explain that the only ingredient not in a cigarette is salt. The rest of the substances contain chemicals that are added to tobacco products, occur naturally in tobacco or are created during the combustion of tobacco products. There are about 4000 chemical compounds contained in tobacco smoke, including over 60 known to cause cancer.

As many as 400 'ingredients' can be added to tobacco and cigarettes by the tobacco industry for purposes such as flavouring, burn enhancement, acidity regulation, nicotine uptake, pest control, colouring, reducing harshness and volume-to-weight manipulation. Some of these additives are known carcinogens and respiratory irritants.

These are then inhaled, along with tobacco, into the lungs when a smoker lights up.

*'Odd One Out' cards*

| | | |
|---|---|---|
| **FLOOR CLEANER** | **BLEACH** | **SUGAR** |
| **ANT POISON** | **SILICONE** | **ARTIFICIAL SWEETENER** |
| **RAT POISON** | **CINNAMON** | **WASHING POWDER** |

| | | |
|---|---|---|
| NAIL POLISH REMOVER | WATER-BASED GLUE | LIQUORICE |
| CHOCOLATE | FILM NEGATIVE | SALT |
| TOBACCO | MOTH BALLS | TAR |

# WORD ASSOCIATION

## Aim

This circle time activity introduces the topic of tobacco products and smoking.

## You will need

- A small ball
- Flipchart and markers

## How to do it

Invite the young people to stand in a circle and give the ball to one person. Explain that they will start the activity.

Write 'SMOKING' in large letters onto the flipchart sheet, displayed where every member of the group can see it.

Explain that when you shout 'Go!' the person holding the ball should call out one word associated with the word 'smoking' before throwing the ball across the circle to another person. The second person should catch the ball and then call out another word associated with smoking, before repeating the action.

Encourage the young people to keep the ball moving and keep the ideas flowing. In the meantime record all of the words that are called out.

If someone doesn't catch the ball then they must think of two words before throwing it on. If anyone cannot think of a word associated with smoking then they should shout 'QUIT SMOKING!' before passing it on.

Keep the momentum going until the young people have run out of words. Congratulate everyone for taking part, and once they are seated show them the list that has been created using their ideas. This list can be used to introduce further activities that raise awareness of the different smoking-related topics identified.

# MAKING DECISIONS ABOUT SMOKING

# EXPLORING ATTITUDES

## *Aim*

To explore young people's attitude to smoking and the sale of cigarettes in a non-confrontational way, encouraging them to say what they really think.

## *You will need*

- Nothing

## *How to do it*

Explain to the group that you are going to read out a series of statements that describe feelings and views about smoking. The area to the left of you is the 'agree' zone, to the right is a 'disagree' zone and in the middle is the 'undecided' zone.

Ask the young people to show you how they feel about the statement you read out by moving to the zone which corresponds most with their opinion. Point out that this is not a test, but rather an exercise to find out what the group thinks. Try to encourage the young people to make their own decisions, rather than following their friends' views.

Leave space between statements to review what the group are saying and make sure that there is an opportunity for the young people to ask questions and debate issues raised.

STATEMENTS

1. People who get cancer through smoking should not get preferential hospital treatment.

2. It is safe to smoke as long as you give up before you are 30.

3. If the government puts up the price of cigarettes enough no one will smoke.

4. Smoking should be made illegal like other addictive drugs.

5. Anti-smoking campaigns just don't work.

6. People who smoke near children should be arrested – it is child abuse.

7. Smoking bans in bars and clubs should be lifted.

8. Not displaying cigarettes in shops will reduce the number of people smoking.

9. All cigarettes should be sold in plain boxes.

10. Advertising cigarettes doesn't encourage smoking.

# MESSAGES

## *Aim*

This activity enables young people to explore the messages that they have received about smoking and tobacco and how this has or hasn't influenced their personal beliefs and decisions.

## *You will need*

- Six pieces of flipchart paper
- Sticky tack
- Coloured markers

## *How to do it*

In advance, take the pieces of flipchart paper and label them 'FRIENDS', 'ADULT YOU LIVE WITH', 'YOUTH WORKER/TEACHER', 'MEDIA'.

Start the activity by explaining that people learn about things from a wide range of sources. Information is given to us and we process it to form our own opinions, beliefs and ideas. These may or may not be heavily influenced by the people giving us the information. Suggest that this includes learning about smoking and tobacco.

Next, stick up the posters around the wall and hand each young person a marker and invite them to move around the room, writing comments, things they learnt or messages they received about smoking from the sources under the different headings. Suggest that these can be recent, things they learnt growing up or things they have learnt through targeted learning; for example, during science or health education lessons.

Now, divide the main group into four and hand each group one of the flipchart sheets to discuss:

1.   What messages are given about smoking?

2.   Are they consistent?

3.   How do these messages affect what we think/believe/do?

4.   How reliable are they?

Allow time for discussion and then invite each group to feed back their findings. In particular, focus on the role of the media and how it affects what young people think or believe about smoking. Does this message differ from the things that parents or teachers say, for example? Is the media powerful enough to influence a person's decision to smoke or not? Pull out comments and record for future sessions.

# DO AS I SAY

## *Aim*

Slip this activity into any session to demonstrate how peer pressure can work within a group and open up discussions about trust.

## *You will need*

- A bowl of small sweets/chocolates/fruit
- A colleague or senior member to act as the 'pressure'

## *How to do it*

Show the young people the bowl of goodies and explain that they are a treat for later. Carry on with your main session, referring back several times to the treats and stressing that nobody must take one until invited later. Try to build a bit of anticipation!

Leave the room on a pretext of getting something, reminding people not to touch the sweets whilst you are gone.

Once you are out of sight, your co-worker or chosen young person should wait a few seconds before casually saying something such as: 'Shall we have a sweet? If we just take one each it won't be noticed!'

They should then pick up the bowl and repeat the suggestion, taking a treat and eating it before passing the bowl around the group. If anyone hesitates they should build on the idea that it will be OK, remind them that the bowl of sweets is for them and pointing out that there is no real reason to wait.

When you come back into the room ignore the bowl at first. Then suddenly pretend to notice that there are treats missing. Ask the young people to be honest and raise their hand if they took one.

Then admit that really this was an exercise in peer pressure. Ask the following questions and facilitate a discussion around the answers:

1. If you took a sweet, what made you decide to do it?

2. If you didn't, what stopped you?

3. How did you feel about your decision once you had eaten or not eaten it?

Answers should include things such as, 'because everyone else did it', and 'because I like what was on offer and the temptation was too great' or 'because I didn't think it would matter'.

Conclude that people are often persuaded to do things, even though they have been told not to, because of all of the above reasons, especially if the person encouraging them is someone they respect, like, admire or are used to complying with.

Suggest that often the first person to offer a cigarette to a young person is a friend or older sibling and the fact that they are doing it, or sanction it, overrides any advice not to do it.

Conclude that peer pressure does not necessarily mean somebody standing over them forcing them with physical pressure to smoke. It is far more likely that the decision will be based on things such as what other people are doing, role models, the situation and things such as whether they think they can do it without being found out.

# FOLLOW ON

## *Aim*

This simple activity demonstrates how non-verbal peer pressure works and opens up discussion.

## *You will need*

- Paper and pens

## *How to do it*

This demonstration of non-verbal peer pressure is easy to facilitate, but does need careful staging to ensure that it looks natural.

Secretly choose a member of your group who is generally confident and unlikely to become upset at being an unwitting volunteer and ask them to leave the room on an 'errand'.

Whilst they are out of the room explain to the rest of the young people that this is an experiment in peer pressure, and the person who has left the room is the subject. Now, instruct everyone to sit on the floor cross-legged or strike a pose. If you have a less able group invite them all to raise an arm or put their hands on their heads. The important point is that everyone should be doing the same.

When the absent member comes back, acknowledge their return, but do not comment on what everyone else is doing, no matter how bizarre! If they ask you directly then just smile and shrug your shoulders or give some other non-committal response.

Watch what happens – if the young person copies what everyone else is doing then explain that this is an example of non-verbal peer pressure. Ask them:

1. Why did you follow the others?

2. Did you consider not copying them?

Point out that nobody told them to follow what the others were doing; they just fell into doing it.

If the young person ignores what everyone else is doing and returns to where they were, then they resisted the pressure to conform. Ask them:

1. Why didn't you do the same as the rest of the group?

2. Why did you do something different?

3. How did that feel?

Review the activity to discuss what happened:

1. Who else would have copied everyone else? Why?

2. Who would have ignored what others were doing? Why?

3. How does it feel to go against the group and be different?

Remark that usually peer pressure is a term used to describe someone putting pressure on someone else to do something wrong, but actually this is not always so. Suggest that when people are with friends, or within most group situations, they tend to fall in with what everyone else is doing: sometimes, as demonstrated by this activity, without even realizing that they are doing it.

# EXPLORING POSITIVE AND NEGATIVE PEER PRESSURE

## Aim

This discussion-based activity enables young people to explore the positive and negative power of collective and peer pressure.

## You will need

- Flipchart paper and markers

## How to do it

Invite the young people to reflect on all of the groups they belong to. This should include friendship groups and families as well as organized groups; for example, sports clubs or uniformed groups such as the Scouts or Guides. Discuss the positive feelings and benefits they get from membership. This could include love, security, shared interests, fun and a sense of 'belonging'.

Now move on to ask:

- Do you behave the same way in a group as you do on your own?

- Do you behave differently with different groups?

Discuss the differences in behaviour, for example, between being at a party with friends and at a family celebration with grandparents. Conclude that most people are multi-faceted and show different sides of themselves in different circumstances. Indicate that psychologists' research suggests people are heavily influenced by the people they spend time with and what they see others doing.

Discuss, in pairs, a time when:

- you were encouraged by others to succeed in something you found challenging

- you felt pressured by others into doing something you believed to be wrong.

Encourage the young people to explore the reasons behind their actions and what informed their final decisions, including what they hoped to gain or feared to lose by their choices.

Invite feedback and record ideas under the headings 'GAIN' and 'LOSE'. So, for example, a 'gain' might be achievement, satisfaction, peer acceptance or status, but by following the crowd you may 'lose' respect, get into trouble, feel guilty or lose the opportunity to act on your values.

Explain that the factors that persuade someone to do, or not do, something can be referred to as both the risk and protective factors that contribute to 'peer pressure'. Whilst belonging to a group can create powerful feelings of safety, protection and value, peer pressure can sway people to engage in less positive behaviour as well, and even get swept along into actions they later regret. This includes decisions about smoking, drinking or taking drugs.

Conclude that whilst it can be hard to go against the crowd, it is important to maintain personal values and remain an individual within a group. Peer pressure, whilst powerful, should not be used as an excuse for making negative choices as everyone has personal responsibility for their decisions and actions, as well as responsibilities to the groups they are a part of.

# MAKING DECISIONS

### Aim

To support young people in looking at the way they make decisions and the factors that influence them.

### You will need

- A copy of the 'Making Decisions' sheet
- Pens

### How to do it

Ask each young person to think of two decisions that they have made recently. These do not have to be major life-changing decisions; for example, it might be what to spend babysitting money on or where to go at the weekend. However, if they have made a big decision recently that they want to share then that is fine too.

Now, ask each person to turn to the person sitting next to them and share the decisions that they have identified.

Invite the group to share any key influences or themes around how the identified decisions were made. Facilitate a short discussion on the way decisions are made. Suggest that most decisions are made in the following ways and write these up on a flipchart sheet where everyone can see.

Decisions are made:

- after listening to friends
- instinctively
- on the spur of the moment
- at the last minute
- after thinking it through.

Now hand out a worksheet to each pair and ask them to think of an example of decision-making for each process. For example, quickly moving your hand away from a hot kettle is an instinctive decision that you do not need to think about, whereas hopefully examination subject options are considered and thought through.

Allow 15–20 minutes depending on the size of the group to think about this and when everyone has finished bring the whole group back together again. Facilitate a feedback session and discuss the plus and minus factors for each decision-making process and individuals' preferred or usual way of making decisions.

Now move on to ask, 'How have you (or would you) made a decision about whether to smoke or not?' Encourage the young people to consider:

1. things that would influence their decision

2. any sources of pressure

3. what would help them to stick to their decision.

Review responses and agree strategies to make healthy decisions and sources of support to help the young people stick to them.

✓

*'Making Decisions' sheet*

| A decision made after listening to friends | |
|---|---|
| Positives | Negatives |
| A decision made by instinct | |
| Positives | Negatives |

✓

| A rushed decision | |
|---|---|
| Positives | Negatives |
| A thought-through decision | |
| Positives | Negatives |

# SMOKING SCALE

### Aim

This sorting game enables young people to explore the reasons why someone may choose to smoke and for the facilitator to challenge ideas in a non-threatening way.

### You will need

- Sets of the 'Smoking Scale' cards

### How to do it

Divide the large group into smaller groups of three or four and hand each small group an envelope containing a set of the 'Smoking Scale' cards.

Explain that the task for each group is to look through the cards, which suggest reasons why a young person might decide to start smoking. When they have had a chance to discuss ideas, they should choose the nine that they think are the most popular reasons and then rank them 1–9. There are three blank cards included so that the young people can use their own ideas too.

The chosen cards should then be laid out to form a diamond, with the card the group feels is most important at the top, graduating down to the least important at the bottom.

When each group has finished their diamond, review the outcomes as a whole group. How similar are different groups' diamonds? Have all the groups identified one important motivation or reason for smoking? Which card came up most in each group? Which motives were completely discarded?

Invite the young people to discuss their choices and challenge some of the ideas on the cards as the debate progresses, introducing the financial, social and health implications of the decision to smoke.

## 'Smoking Scale' cards

These cards show 12 reasons why young people might choose to start smoking. There are two spare cards for your own ideas.

| | | |
|---|---|---|
| To feel good about themselves | To look older than they are | Because all their friends smoke |
| Because their parents smoke | Because they see cigarettes on display in supermarkets and shops | Because they are stressed and it helps them relax |

| | | |
|---|---|---|
| Because they want to rebel against their family/ friends/school rules | Because they like the smell | To experiment |
| Because they want to smoke it with cannabis | Because their friends encourage them to | Because it looks good |
| | | |

# TAKING RISKS

## Aims

This activity promotes discussion about risk-taking behaviour, reducing risks and making healthy choices.

## You will need

- A set of 'Taking Risks' cards
- Two A4 sheets, labelled 'VERY RISKY' and 'NOT VERY RISKY'

## How to do it

Ask the young people to sit in a circle and hand each a 'Taking Risks' card, asking them not to share what is on their card.

Place one of the A4 sheets on one side of the circle where everyone can see it and the other on the opposite side.

In turn, invite the young people to read out what is on their card and then place it where they think it should go between the two poles. They should then explain their decision.

Set a rule that at this stage only the person who has the card can speak or make the decision, but there will be a chance later to challenge the choice.

Go around the circle until all the cards have been used and then ask if everyone is happy with where the cards are placed on the floor. If anyone wants to move a card they now can but they must explain why they want to move it.

Once all the cards are in place, facilitate a discussion around where the cards are placed and why the young people consider them a greater or lesser risk. Point out that some risks can be reduced. For example, riding a motorbike may be more risky than driving a car, but one way to reduce the risk would be always to wear a well-fitting crash helmet and ride the bike carefully.

Make sure that you explain that all risks are relative; for example, some are likely to cause damage to health, some may not be very serious while some may be very dangerous. Some effects of risky behaviour are immediate, but some may not become obvious for years. For example, smoking may not cause instant health problems, but could cause serious long-term problems later on in life.

Suggest that of all the risks included, the one that carries the greatest likelihood of both short-term and long-term harm is smoking. Discuss where they have placed it on the scale, and the reasons for it, using the opportunity to inform the young people about the social, health and financial impact that smoking can have on an individual.

✓

*'Taking Risks' cards*

| | | |
|---|---|---|
| Crossing the road | Sleeping less than seven hours a night | Riding a motorbike |
| Eating lots of fried food and chips | Not taking regular exercise | Smoking |
| Binge-drinking alcohol | Having unprotected sex | Not wearing a seat belt |

| | | |
|---|---|---|
| Getting into a car when the driver has been drinking alcohol | Being very overweight | Vomiting after eating to diet |
| Doing a bungee jump | Walking alone home at night | Lying to parents/carers |
| Hanging around with young people who are in trouble with the police | Missing school | Rock climbing |

| Playing rugby | Fighting |
|---|---|

# SMOKING AND THE LAW

## Aim

This activity provokes discussion and assesses knowledge within the group about the legalities of buying and using tobacco products.

## You will need

- Information about smoking laws
- A copy of the voting sheet for each young person
- A blank copy of the voting sheet enlarged on a photocopier and pasted to the wall
- Pens
- A cardboard or shoe box painted black and sealed with a slit in the top large enough to post the 'votes' into

## *How to do it*

Hand out a copy of the voting sheet folded in half and a pen to each young person.

Explain that this is a democratic election – that is, one person, one voting sheet – to consider the laws about the buying, selling and use of tobacco products. Stress that the voting will be anonymous and that although you will be inviting discussion after the votes have been counted, at this stage the votes should be cast privately. The votes will be counted and, as in real political elections, the 'first-past-the-post' system will be used to determine the results.

Introduce the cardboard 'ballot box' and ask the young people to look at their sheets, placing a cross in the boxes that correspond with the votes they wish to make. Each person should choose three laws to vote for.

When all votes have been cast, invite the young people to tally up the number of votes against each group and record the results onto the large voting sheet on the wall.

Review the results with the group and compare with the information about existing laws. Ask the young people to explain their votes, particularly where there are differences between the actual laws and the rules that the young people would like to have in place.

## Voting sheet

Place a cross (X) in the box to cast your vote

|  | YES | NO |
|---|---|---|
| Smoking in cars should be made illegal | | |
| If a person is caught smoking in a public place in charge of a child they should be arrested | | |
| The smoking ban in pubs and clubs should be lifted | | |
| Smoking in hospital grounds should be made illegal | | |
| Smoking in the street should be made illegal | | |
| People should be fined for dropping cigarette butts in the street | | |
| The legal age to buy cigarettes should be raised to 21 | | |
| If a young person under the age of 18 is caught smoking their parent should be fined | | |

| | YES | NO |
|---|---|---|
| Any shop caught selling tobacco products (including cigarette papers) to a person under the age of 18 should have their licence to sell tobacco taken away | | |
| It should be made illegal to smoke anywhere but your own home | | |
| If a person is admitted to hospital for a smoking-related disease or illness they should pay for treatment | | |
| The legal age to buy tobacco should be reduced to 16 | | |

# THE PRESSURE IS ON

## Aim

This is a role-play activity where young people take turns at trying to influence a decision made, in order to build assertiveness skills.

## You will need

- Paper and pens
- Copies of the 'Influencing' scenarios
- Clock

## How to do it

Divide the young people into groups of three. Explain that during this activity everyone will have the opportunity to be the 'Influencer', 'Influenced' and 'Observer'.

Ask for volunteers from each group to be the Observer for the first round and give them paper and pens to make notes.

Explain that the task for the person who is playing the part of the Influencer is to spend three minutes trying to persuade the other young person to go along with what they want them to do. They can apply as much pressure as they like to make this happen, but no physical force should be used.

The Observer should watch what happens, including verbal and non-verbal communication, and make notes to feed back afterwards. After three minutes call time and ask the Observer to share what they saw happening.

Swap roles and repeat the exercise, with a new scenario each time, until everyone has experienced being pressured and putting pressure on someone.

Review using these questions:

1.  How easy is it to resist face-to-face pressure to do something? Why?

2.  What strategies worked best to remain assertive?

3.  How easy is it to be assertive in real life?

4.  In what areas of your life do you feel most confident in being assertive, and which the least confident?

## 'Influencing' scenarios

| | |
|---|---|
| Persuade the other person to stay out later than they are allowed to | Persuade the other person to lend you money |
| Persuade the other person to have a cigarette with you | Persuade the other person to fill out a job application for you |
| Persuade the other person to lie for you | Persuade the other person to break their diet and eat a big cream cake |
| Persuade the other person to buy a DVD off you | Persuade the other person to come out with you tonight |
| Persuade the other person to tell you some gossip about a mutual friend | Persuade the other person to try to buy alcohol illegally |

# 50 WAYS TO SAY 'NO!'

## *Aim*

This exercise demonstrates how body language plays a major part in communication.

## *You will need*

- Nothing

## *How to do it*

Invite the young people either to stand or sit in a large circle. This is important, as they need to be able to see each other.

Open the game by explaining that communication is not just about speaking and listening. Whilst it is really important to speak clearly and listen actively – that is, not jump to conclusions or 'second guess' what someone is going to say – body language and tone are just as vital. Suggest that changing these by, for example, making eye contact, hand gestures, smiling or frowning can change the whole context of the conversation and meaning. Offer an example to show what you mean – the word 'whatever' works well!

The game is to go around the circle as many times as possible to demonstrate different ways to say 'NO!' After each person's turn the rest of the group should guess the mood or meaning from the tone of voice and body language used. For example, shouting could be angry or a cry of amazement; you could beg someone to stop or encourage them not to stop.

See how many ways it can be said – congratulate the group and conclude that the power of body language is great, or try again using a new word.

# TAX ME

## Aim

This activity encourages young people to explore how much tax smokers pay on each carton of cigarettes, and the ethics of taxation.

## You will need

- Local figures for tax levied on tobacco and cigarettes
- Sticky notes
- Worksheets and pens for each person

## How to do it

Start by suggesting that the average smoker in both the UK and USA is thought to smoke about 15 cigarettes a day. That is four to six packs a week. A study in London, UK gave the figure that an average smoker in Britain spends £92,000 on cigarettes in his lifetime, in number terms that's 373,300 cigarettes.[3] Conclude that this makes the tobacco industry a lot of money each year.

Suggest that the tobacco giants are not the only people making money out of smokers. Give each participant a sticky note and ask them to write on it how much they think is paid to the government in tax on each packet of cigarettes. Invite people to call out their ideas and stick the notes somewhere that everyone can see. Once everyone has contributed, cluster the notes into similar prices and reflect on the scale suggested.

Then offer the following. According to the Campaign for Tobacco-Free Kids in America, states currently charge an average of $1.47 in taxes on each pack of cigarettes.[4] In the UK every cigarette nets the government around 38p – so on a £7.50 packet of 20, the government pockets around £5.83.[5]

Divide the young people into small groups and give one of the debate points below to each group to argue. Allow 20 minutes for them to come up with arguments to support the given point of view and then facilitate a whole-group discussion, inviting each group to present their ideas in turn.

---

3   www.quitspeed.com/2006/01/19/how-many-cigarettes-does-the-average-regular-normal-smoker-smoke/.

4   www.tobaccofreekids.org.

5   www.thisismoney.co.uk/money/news/article-1633429/Calculator-tax-pay-beer-wine-cigarettes-spirits.html.

### DEBATE VIEW 1

Smokers cause their own illness, so it is only fair that they should pay high tax on the cigarettes.

### DEBATE VIEW 2

People should be grateful to smokers. The high tax they pay on cigarettes contributes to other things that benefit everyone.

### DEBATE VIEW 3

The government should raise tax on cigarettes even higher. That way it would stop people smoking.

### DEBATE VIEW 4

Governments are greedy. They know people are never going to stop smoking so tobacco is an easy target for tax increases.

Once each group has presented their argument, spend time discussing which point of view the young people agree with most, and the reasons why.

Conclude by suggesting that next time they see someone with a cigarette they should remember where so much of the money is going, and the real cost of tobacco.

# COUNTING THE COST

## Aim

To encourage young people to consider how much smoking costs and what money spent on cigarettes could be used for.

## You will need

- Paper and pens
- Scissors and glue
- Holiday brochures, catalogues (clothes, sports equipment, consumer products, etc.)
- Local costs of a packet of cigarettes

## How to do it

Remind the young people that it is estimated that the average adult smoker smokes between 13 and 16 cigarettes a day, or four to six cartons a week. Give out the information about local costs, and work out how much this would be per week and per year using the average smoking statistics.

If the young people are smokers, help them work out what they are spending on tobacco too.

Now, distribute the paper, pens, scissors, glue and catalogues, etc. Invite the young people to look through and see what could be bought by choosing not to spend money on smoking.

They should cut out pictures of the things that really appeal to them, working out if they would be affordable by saving the money from giving up smoking. Encourage them to make a collage each, writing motivational statements around the things that they want to spur them on.

Suggest that everyone takes their collage home and displays it somewhere that is prominent. Every time they feel the urge to spend money on tobacco they should be reminded that their goal is achievable.

Make regular time to discuss and reinforce goals and celebrate successes, even small ones. Remind them that each cigarette less is one step towards getting what they want.

# HEALTH

# SMOKING BOTTLE

## Aim

This is an outdoors group activity to use as part of a health session around smoking and the effects it has on the body. It demonstrates how tar collects in the lungs when nicotine is inhaled, using a smoking bottle.

## You will need

- A filter cigarette
- Sticky tack
- Cotton wool
- A large, empty, clean, dry, clear, plastic bottle
- Matches
- Leaflets for support groups and/or giving-up information

## How to do it

To prepare for the activity, make the smoking bottle. Do this by taking the empty plastic bottle and pushing cotton wool into it until you have a good sized wad covering the bottom of the bottle. Next take the cigarette and place it into the neck, holding it in place with some sticky tack.

Due to legal restrictions of where you can and can't smoke this activity needs to be facilitated outside.

Open the activity by explaining that the aim is to look at smoking, in particular cigarettes, and the effect it can have on your health. You may want to facilitate a short discussion or conduct a quick poll to see how many of the young people smoke or have ever tried a cigarette. Refer to your group contract and the confidentiality rule that was agreed.

Bring out the smoking bottle and ask for a volunteer. Invite the volunteer to light the cigarette in the top of the bottle. Once it is alight, ask the young person to squeeze the sides of the bottle gently to simulate lungs inhaling and exhaling.

Pass the bottle around the group, inviting everyone to have a go. As the bottle is passed, ask the group to comment on any changes they see to the cotton wool. It will gradually turn brown as tar from the cigarette is collected in the fibres.

Review what has happened, explaining that this is similar to the effect smoking has on a person's lungs.

Answer any questions that arise, hand out leaflets and ensure that the young people know where they can go for further help or support if necessary.

# WARNING LABELS

## Aim

The aim of this activity is to raise awareness of the health warning labels present on cigarette boxes and explore the impact of them.

## You will need

- Photocopies of the warning labels on cigarette cartons (or images available online)
- Pictures of cigarette cartons (cut out)
- Sticky labels (the right size to fit onto the picture of the cigarette box)
- Pens

## How to do it

Divide the young people into small discussion groups and give each group a selection of warning labels from tobacco products to discuss. Explain why the labels are required and the impact that governments across the world hope that they will have in reducing the number of people smoking.

Invite the young people to read and analyze the warnings and discuss the following questions:

- Do you think people will stop smoking after reading the labels? Why or why not?

- Are the labels effective in preventing people from starting to smoke tobacco products? Why or why not?

Invite each group to feed back their conclusions and invite further discussion.

Next, set each group the task of creating a new warning label for cigarettes that they think clearly describes the risks of use and encourages people to stop or never start smoking. Hand out the pictures of the cigarette packaging and sticky labels so that they can design their new label and stick it in place.

Invite each group to present their alternative warning label, explaining their design and the hoped-for impact, and then create a display of them to inform other young people of the risks that smoking poses.

# IT COULD BE YOU

## Aim

This activity raises awareness about smoking-related illness and diseases.

## You will need

- Small pieces of paper rolled up and secured to look like cigarettes

## How to do it

To prepare, make fake cigarettes by writing the following messages onto white paper and then rolling and sticking using a light water-based glue:

1. You will smoke from the age of 14 until you die peacefully in your sleep aged 101.

2. You will never smoke, but will develop a hereditary form of cancer in your late 40s.

3. You will never smoke, but will develop cancer due to the passive or second-hand smoke of your partner.

4. You will never smoke, but will suffer bronchitis due to your parents smoking around you.

5. You will become a heavy smoker and develop cancer of the larynx (voice box), which needs to be removed in your 50s.

6. You will smoke whilst pregnant and your baby will be born underweight as a consequence.

7. You try smoking but decide that the health risks are too great and never smoke again.

8. You smoke and your partner dumps you because they don't like the smell of tobacco on your breath.

9. You start smoking but want to be a professional sportsperson so give up with support from your youth worker.

10. You smoke occasionally and think that it won't damage your health, but along with an unhealthy diet and excessive alcohol it contributes to you developing heart disease in your late 20s.

11. You smoke and have developed a smoker's cough in the mornings, which if left untreated will develop into emphysema (lung disease).

12. You will never smoke as you think it is a dirty and disgusting habit.

13. You smoke unfiltered roll-up cigarettes to avoid all the chemicals in ready-made cigarettes, and develop terminal lung cancer just before your 40th birthday.

14. You smoke and by your 30th birthday you have fine smoker's wrinkles around your eyes, nose and mouth.

15. You will never smoke as one of your parents died of a smoking-related disease.

Start the activity by informing the young people that according to leading UK charity Cancer Research, 'In the UK, smoking kills five times more people than road accidents, overdoses, murder, suicide and HIV all put together. The good news is that most of these deaths are preventable, by giving up smoking in time.'[6]

Hand each person a fake cigarette and explain that this cigarette holds the key to their future. They now have a choice:

1. Accept their fate and keep the cigarette.

2. Swap their fate with another member of the group.

---

6  http://info.cancerresearchuk.org/healthyliving/smokingandtobacco/smoking-and-cancer.

Allow time for people to swap, inviting them to share the reasons for their decision.

Call time and invite everyone to sit down, unwrap their cigarette and reveal their fate. Next encourage each person to share what is inside their cigarette paper, and how they feel about it. Suggest that these illnesses are no respecter of person, status or situation, meaning that no smoker can possibly know when they first start smoking what the health outcome will be for them. Not all smokers will definitely get cancer, but smoking greatly increases the risk of this disease.

Now ask: 'If you really had a way of knowing your fate, would this affect your decision to smoke or not smoke?'

Point out that whilst no one can foresee the future in such clarity, statistics and the laws of probability suggest that the fates outlined on the papers are not far from the truth for some smokers. Smokers are, on average, much more likely to get cancer than non-smokers and have a reduced life expectancy.

# SMOKING AND THE BODY

## Aim

This activity raises awareness of the impact of smoking on the inside and outside of the body.

## You will need

- Large sheets of paper or a roll of lining paper
- Marker pens

## How to do it

Divide the young people into three groups and hand paper and markers to each group. Either invite a volunteer to lay down whilst a group member draws around them to produce a life size human outline, or if that is inappropriate then ask a volunteer to draw a large gingerbread person onto the paper.

Start off by suggesting that smoking can cause several deadly illnesses, which can develop quickly or slowly, including the one that they have probably already heard of, cancer. Point out that some of these can even have no symptoms at all until in a very advanced stage.

Tell each group that they have three minutes to discuss and then mark on the relevant part of the body the effects that smoking can have inside the body.

This should include heart disease, lung and oesophageal cancer, chronic lung disease, and cancer of the bladder, kidney and pancreas. Tobacco can also contribute to the development of cancer of the gum, mouth, larynx and oesophagus and increase the risks of diseases such as bronchitis and emphysema.

An additional problem that they may not be aware of is erectile dysfunction, where the blood supply to the penis becomes limited leading to even young men having problems maintaining an erection.

Call time, and pass the papers onto the next group. Now, ask the young people to write or draw on them all of the effects of smoking to the outside of the body. This can include premature ageing to the face, smoking lines around the mouth, smelly breath, nicotine-stained fingers, etc.

Once again, call time and pass the papers to the third group. This time invite them to read all of the comments and ideas already written, and then give them three minutes to write down as many reasons as possible why people might choose to start smoking.

Finally, call time and pass the papers back to their original groups and invite them to review what has been written.

Facilitate a discussion that considers their findings and asks:

1. With so much known about the health risks of smoking tobacco (in any form), why do people still choose to start?

2. What has influenced your decision to smoke or not smoke?

3. If you met your dream boy/girl, would it matter to you if they smoked? Why or why not?

# LONG TERM/SHORT TERM

## *Aim*

The aim of this activity is to consider both the long-term and short-term effects of smoking on the body and general health.

## *You will need*

- Large sheets of paper and markers
- Sets of the 'Long Term/Short Term' cards

## *How to do it*

Divide the young people into small groups and give paper, markers and a set of cards to each group.

Set the task off by asking them to draw two large overlapping circles in the middle of the page (a Venn diagram). One circle should be marked 'Long Term', the other 'Short Term' and the overlapping area 'Both'.

The task for each group is to discuss each card and then place it in the correct circle after gauging whether it is a long-term or short-term health risk. If they believe it to be both then it should be placed in the middle.

Once all of the cards have been placed, rotate between groups, inviting each one to explain their choice, and discussing their decisions as you go along.

Conclude that, as well as social consequences, such as having to stand outside in the cold to smoke and having less money to spend on other things, smokers run the risk of both short-term and long-term health problems. Even if a smoker is lucky enough to avoid these it can be impossible not to smell of stale smoke and ash on clothes, hair and skin – even if the cigarettes have been smoked outside.

End by pointing out that, by giving up, smokers can take responsibility for their own health and that of anyone they smoke around, and reduce these risks.

*'Long Term/Short Term'* cards

| LONG TERM | SHORT TERM | BOTH |
|---|---|---|
| Bad skin | Smelly clothes | Bad breath |
| Wrinkles around the mouth | Smelly hair | Yellow teeth |

✓

| LONG TERM | SHORT TERM | BOTH |
|---|---|---|
| Slower recovery time from common illnesses | Increased risk of coughs, colds, flu and bronchitis | Stained fingers |
| Reduced healing for injuries such as damaged tendons or ligaments | Dizziness | Shortness of breath |
| Throat, lung, stomach and bladder cancer | | Decreased blood circulation |

| LONG TERM | SHORT TERM | BOTH |
|---|---|---|
| Poor circulation | | Reduced sports ability |
| Decreased bone density | | Increased heart rate |
| Decreased fertility | | |

✓

| LONG TERM | SHORT TERM | BOTH |
|---|---|---|
| Heart disease | | |
| Stroke | | |
| Emphysema (lung disease) | | |

# MYTHS AND FACTS

## *Aim*

This activity provides an opportunity for young people to give and receive information and check out each others' knowledge about tobacco products and smoking.

## *You will need*

- Internet access and/or information leaflets about tobacco and smoking
- Paper and pens

## *How to do it*

Divide the young people into two teams, with up to six people in each. If you are working with a larger number of young people, then create more teams.

Explain that there are many rumours and stories spread about smoking and the dangers of tobacco products. Suggest that in order to be able to make an informed decision about whether to smoke or not it is important to find out which of these stories are facts and which are myths.

Set each team the task of researching 12 'facts' to ask the other team. All of the information will be presented as 'facts', but not all of them will be correct. For example:

- Tobacco is a drug – FACT.
- All smokers will get lung cancer – MYTH.

Explain that they have 30 minutes for research and can use the internet or leaflets provided, stressing that any information that is being presented as truth must come from a reputable source.

Show the young people how to facilitate their facts as a 'feet first' activity. Invite a group spokesperson to read a statement about tobacco. After the statement is read, members of the opposing team should move to a predetermined corner of the room if they believe the statement is a myth; to another corner of the room if they believe the statement is a fact; or remain in the centre of the room if they are unsure. The team scores a point for every team member who gets the correct answer.

Write up the final score and then swap roles so that the second team can facilitate their 12 'facts'.

The team with the most points wins the game!

# CELEBRITIES AND IMAGE

## *Aim*

This activity raises awareness of the media's role in defining attractiveness and how media images can affect personal attitudes and beliefs about smoking.

## *You will need*

- Pictures of a range of celebrities
- Online access to research celebrities who smoke

## *How to do it*

Prepare sets of pictures of celebrities popular with young people, some who smoke and some who don't. Try to include those with 'clean' public images and those more famous for their 'bad' behaviour. Make sure that none are actually pictured with a cigarette or cigar.

Divide the young people into small groups and hand each group a set of pictures. The young people should decide which celebrities they think are smokers and which aren't, based solely on how they look. Play this as a game and award each team a point for every correct answer.

As you go through the answers, ask the young people to explain why they chose certain celebrities and not others. Are their answers based on knowledge, for example, they have seen a picture of the celebrity smoking, or are they based on what they think a smoker looks like? Explore this concept as far as possible.

Next ask the young people to go through the pile of smokers and define some of the things they are famous for. For example, this could be their youthful looks, body size or 'cool' image as well as actual achievements. Continue the discussion, asking the young people to consider how much they think celebrities and celebrity culture influence people and their decisions.

Conclude that the media clearly promotes what is deemed attractive, and ordinary people often measure their own attractiveness against it.

Go on to ask the young people to name some of the detrimental effects that smoking can have on health in terms of physical appearances and note down suggestions. Facilitate a discussion that considers:

1. Smokers can have yellowish teeth due to staining caused by nicotine in cigarettes; how does this fit with the money spent by celebrities to have a 'Hollywood' smile?

2. Smoking can cause hair thinning and in some cases hair loss; in celebrity-land is having lovely hair an important attribute?

3. Most celebrities seem to want to stay as youthful looking as possible; yet smoking is proven to cause rapid skin ageing.

Suggest to the young people that the media does not show this less attractive side of smoking in their eagerness to show celebrities as 'perfect'. However, if they really wanted to encourage young people not to smoke they could influence choices by showing those stars who do smoke with 'smoking' lines around their mouth or nicotine-stained fingers, etc. Invite discussion about the validity of this statement and encourage suggestions of other ways that the media could show a truer picture.

# WORKING OUT THE PROS AND CONS OF QUITTING

## Aim

This individual activity encourages those planning to give up smoking to reflect on what could happen as a consequence of their decision.

## You will need

- A 'Quit' sheet and pen
- Information about local support

## How to do it

Introduce the 'Quit' sheet and explain that every smoker's experience of giving up is likely to be different. Suggest that this activity will enable them to reflect on what might change as a consequence of their decision.

As the young person completes the worksheet, facilitate a discussion that considers:

- EXTREMES – What is the worst thing that could happen if you don't quit smoking?

- LOOK BACK – What were things like before you smoked?

- LOOK FORWARD – What will they be like after you give up?

- EXPLORE GOALS – Look at any discrepancy between important goals and the behaviour, for example, wanting to be good at sport but continuing to smoke, which is likely to have an adverse effect on performance.

At the bottom, encourage them to set a realistic goal that can be reviewed and added to regularly. Give the worksheet to the young person to take home and work on, and keep to use when you next meet.

✓

*'Quit' sheet*

|  | **Pros** | **Cons** |
|---|---|---|
| **Change** | | |
| **No change** | | |

# GIVING UP WALK-THROUGH

## *Aim*

This activity introduces young people to the cycle of giving up smoking. It considers triggers and identifies support networks to help people stick to decisions made.

## *You will need*

- A copy of the cycle drawn onto several sheets of flipchart paper stuck together
- Flipchart and marker pens

## *How to do it*

To prepare, draw the following cycle onto several sheets of flipchart paper stuck together to create one large sheet.

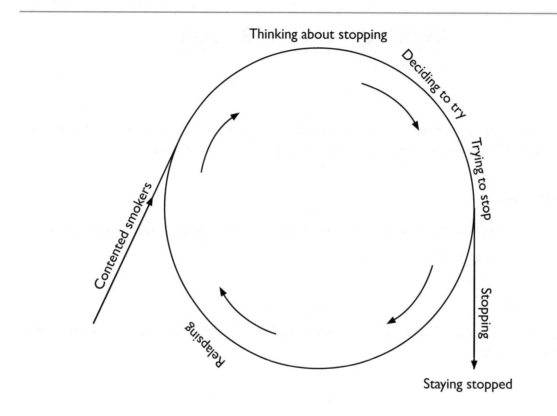

Lay the sheet on the floor and introduce it to the young people, explaining that this is the process that most smokers go through once they decide to quit.

Ask for a volunteer to walk through the process, stopping at each stage to ask the following questions:

- Why might a smoker start to think about quitting? Answers might include finances, wanting to be healthier, other friends quitting or not wanting to be addicted.

- What might trigger the decision to stop? Answers might include being set a challenge, National No Smoking Day, or no longer enjoying tobacco.

- What support might someone need when they are trying to stop? Suggestions might include having someone to support them or a goal to work towards.

- What triggers might make someone smoke again? This could include stress, other people smoking around them, not seeing any immediate benefits or trigger situations such as after a meal or the smell of coffee.

Point out that if a smoker relapses that does not mean that they will not be successful next time. It is important to be positive about the length of time they were smoke-free, and set a date to try again.

Once they have stopped for a set period of time how could they celebrate? Ideas might include spending the money that they have saved by not smoking on something they really want.

Conclude that people might go around the circle several times before they finally manage to quit, but the financial, health and social benefits of being smoke-free are worth trying for.

# MARKETING AND THE ROLE OF THE MEDIA

# LOGOS AND BRANDING

## Aim

This short activity introduces the power of branding and considers marketing that targets young people.

## You will need

- Flipchart and markers
- Pictures of cigarette cartons

## How to do it

Divide the main group into small teams of five to six young people. Hand each team a sheet of flipchart paper and a selection of markers. Now, set them the task to draw as many logos for companies or products as they can think of in three minutes. For example, one of the most recognized symbols in the world is the 'Golden Arches' of McDonald's; another is the globally famous Coca Cola logo.

Ask each team to share their sheet, awarding a point for each logo, and congratulating the team with the most. Then as a whole group ask which logos they think specifically appeal to young people and why.

Next, bring out the pictures of cigarette packs and distribute them amongst the groups. Ask the young people to consider the suggestion that even though in many countries, including the UK, there is a ban on all cigarette advertising, tobacco companies design the packaging of their products to appeal to specific groups of people. Even established brands regularly employ advertising agencies, who fiercely compete for the lucrative contracts, to overhaul their 'corporate look' to make it attractive to new consumers without losing old ones.

Ask the young people to look at the packaging and discuss the following:

1.  Is the packaging targeted at a specific group (e.g. women, younger people)?

2.  How? What messages does it give?

3.  What words are used to describe the cigarettes? For example, 'light', 'mild' or 'low tar'. What do these imply?

4.  Does the packet give useful information about the long-term or short-term effects of tobacco use?

Facilitate a discussion that takes points from each group and record conclusions.

# ADVERTISING – GETTING THE MESSAGE

## Aim

This activity introduces young people to the idea that until 2002 the tobacco industry could openly advertise cigarettes in magazines, on TV and at the movies and sets them the task of creating an advertisement that reflects the truth about smoking.

## You will need

- Copies of 'Golden Age of Hollywood' cigarette advertisements (available from www.smokefreemovies.ucsf.edu) or more recent adverts from www.trinketsandtrash. org that has a library of tobacco products and tobacco industry marketing material
- Flipchart and markers

## How to do it

Set the scene by talking about popular culture and the role that the media plays in people's lives. Suggest that although the celebrity culture, where people become famous for living their lives on TV, could be seen as a 21st century invention, the public fascination for news about their idols is not so new. Movie magazines and Hollywood stars endorsing products have been around a long time. David Beckham and Girls Aloud may be advertising underwear today, but back in the Golden Age of Hollywood (between 1927 and 1951) movie stars endorsed everything, including cigarettes.

Divide the main group into threes or fours and hand out the adverts that you have printed off. Allow ten minutes for discussion, asking the group to record their views onto a flipchart sheet.

1.  How is the sponsor trying to get people to buy or want the cigarettes?

2.  What messages are the movie stars giving?

3.  Who is the intended audience for this ad?

4.  Do you think that seeing these adverts encouraged people to try smoking?

Facilitate a feedback session, encouraging each group to share their views and concluding that tobacco advertising suggests a lifestyle or personal qualities that people might aspire to. Explain that although tobacco companies are no longer allowed to openly advertise cigarettes or any other tobacco products in the UK, elsewhere in the world they still can and do.

Divide the young people into small groups and explain that their task now is to devise a 'truth-telling' TV advert for cigarettes. Encourage them to storyboard their ideas and develop a short scene that includes all members of the group. This can be humorous, hard-hitting or news style – the choice is up to each group to make it as engaging and factual as possible.

Allow 15–20 minutes for the groups to practise their adverts and then invite each group to perform their advert in front of the rest of the young people. Lead a round of applause after each performance and invite questions and discussions.

# LEARNING THE LANGUAGE

## *Aim*

This activity explores the meaning behind the words often used by tobacco companies to promote cigarettes and tobacco products.

## *You will need*

- Large sheets of paper
- Markers

## *How to do it*

Divide the young people into small groups and hand each a large sheet of paper with one of the following words written on it:

- Mild
- Slim

- Rich
- Smooth
- Light.

Their task is to devise an advertising campaign for a product (real or imaginary) that they think fits the descriptive word allocated to them. The only rule is that the product they choose should reflect the meaning of the word. Allow 10–15 minutes for the groups to devise their ad or commercial.

Invite each group to share their 'product', explaining the thinking behind their decisions as well as the advert. After the presentations are finished, suggest that these adjectives are the descriptive words often used in cigarette marketing and advertising. Lead a whole-group discussion that considers the following:

1. Do these words really describe the attributes of cigarettes? Are they accurate, fair, truthful and complete?

2. Why might advertisers think that these adjectives will sell tobacco products?

3. What images do the words conjure up? For example, 'light' might give the impression that these cigarettes or cigars are not as bad for people's health as other brands.

Finally, ask the young people to think of more appropriate words to describe cigarettes and record the ideas to display later.

# THE GREAT DEBATE

## Aim

This whole-group discussion enables young people to research how the tobacco industry promotes its merchandise at points of sale and debate the strategies currently under discussion to stop this.

## You will need

- Copies of the 'Discussion Points' sheet
- Flipchart and markers
- Online access (optional)

## How to do it

Open the activity by suggesting that although direct advertising by tobacco companies has been banned in the UK since 2002, marketing companies are still employed to find alternative ways to promote products in creative ways that directly target new smokers to replace existing consumers who have either quit or died. Go on to point out that one of the largest target markets for this is young people. This is a worldwide multi-million pound or dollar business with advertising agencies hotly competing to secure contracts with the big tobacco companies.

Divide the main group into two (if you have a group of more than 20 then split them into four groups). Explain that one of the few places that tobacco companies can promote their brands is at the point of sale, that is, the cabinet the cigarettes are kept in, price tags, etc.

Hand out the two opposing discussion points, one to each group, and set them the task of discussing and formulating arguments to support that view. Distribute a flipchart and markers so they can make notes. If you have online access, the young people can research this further to help support their viewpoint.

Each group will need to nominate a speaker(s) and plan how they are going to argue their point.

Set up the room with half the chairs on one side and half on the other, facing each other. Invite each group to sit behind their spokesperson(s) and then in turn make their argument. Once both sides have been heard, facilitate a debate that encourages questions and challenges any claims made.

Additional points to raise might be:

1.  Tobacco companies clearly believe their advertising works, otherwise they would not invest millions in it.

2.  This form of marketing is just within the law and is currently under review.

3.  In other places in the world cigarette companies still promote their brands at music festivals, bars and clubs that attract large numbers of young people.

Finally, facilitate a simple vote to see which point of view has the most support. Each person has two votes: first for the argument that they think was presented best (this will allow for them all to vote for themselves!); and second for the argument that they support, having heard both sides.

*'Discussion Points' sheet*

**GROUP 1**

This form of marketing is morally wrong as it encourages people to smoke and increases brand loyalty.

All cigarettes and tobacco should come in plain brown boxes and be sold from under the counter rather than being on public display.

That would make it harder to know where to buy cigarettes, stop subliminal advertising and reduce the sales of tobacco products.

**GROUP 2**

This is a perfectly justified form of marketing that cannot possibly encourage people to smoke.

If you choose to smoke then you should not be made to feel like you are doing something wrong, or have it made more difficult to know where to buy the products.

Hiding cigarettes away and packaging them in plain boxes will make them seem more exciting and actually encourage more young people to experiment.

# SMOKING ON TV

## Aim

This activity considers the ways that smoking is portrayed in soap operas and the messages given to children and young people.

## You will need

- Sheet of soap images
- Access to the internet
- Flipchart and markers

## How to do it

To prepare for the activity, go online and find photos of characters in popular soap operas who smoke. Print them off and cut them out.

At the session, show the young people the photos that you have selected. Once they have seen them all, divide into small groups and hand each group a selection of characters. The group should discuss and record the following:

1. Describe the type of characters that smoke tobacco.

2. Are the smokers in the majority or the minority?

3. Do they smoke during particular times in the plot? If so, what reasons are given?

4. Do they use any smoking paraphernalia (e.g. lighters or matches) as props?

5. Should smoking be shown in soap operas?

Encourage the young people to consider the gender, age, health, popularity and social status of the smokers.

Invite each group to feed back their conclusions, exploring any messages received; for example, characters smoking when they are stressed or upset to feel better. Point out that a popular UK soap aimed at young people, Hollyoaks, has a no-smoking policy that is strictly enforced, so that no characters smoke. Encourage the young people to consider why this might be and the positive messages that it gives to young people who are the target audience.

Facilitate a show of hands to see who thinks that smoking should be shown in soap operas, asking the young people to take into consideration facts such as the time that most soaps are shown as well as health issues. Display the photos and flipchart sheets along with the results of your poll.

*Sources:* ASH Response to the DCMS Consultation on Product Placement on Television – December 2009; www.ashaust.org.su.

# SMOKING AND MUSIC

### Aim

This activity considers the tobacco companies' relationship with music events and asks young people to devise a Festival Charter based on their beliefs and values around smoking in public places, sponsorship and advertising.

### You will need

- Paper and pens

### How to do it

Start the activity by asking which young people, if any, have been to an outdoor music event or festival. Encourage them to share experiences and name some of the big national events, concluding that thousands of people, including young adults, flock to the major festivals to enjoy the music regardless of the weather. Many of the festivals promote a family atmosphere and have stalls and activities for younger members of the audience to enjoy as well.

Move on to ask the group if any of them have noticed who sponsors these events and the individual stages. Explain that companies see the festivals as a great opportunity to advertise their products directly to those that they think are most likely to buy them. Go on to suggest that this includes tobacco companies.

Explain that as restrictions on tobacco advertising increasingly limit promotions, music marketing has become an important vehicle to shape brand image, generate brand recognition and promote tobacco. For example, Imperial Tobacco, through its Rizla brand, has sponsored stages at many of the major festivals. Another way of promoting specific brands at festivals has been to produce special promotional packs that include tobacco, papers and a lighter. In this way the tobacco industry can reach out to its target audience without breaking any laws.

In addition, the UK smoking ban does not apply to outside festivals so people are able to smoke freely. This includes the musicians and singers onstage, and there is video footage showing well-known stars smoking.

Divide the young people into groups of six and ask them to discuss the following statements, which offer conflicting viewpoints:

1. As festivals are outdoors it is right that the same smoking rules don't apply.

2. Festivals that encourage children and are advertised as suitable for families have a responsibility to keep the tobacco companies out.

3. Performers at festivals should be positive role models to festival-goers and not smoke.

4. Tobacco companies should continue to sponsor music events.

From here, they should devise a Festival Charter, that has no more than ten points on it, to create a positive, healthy environment for everyone to enjoy live music. Hand out paper and pens to record suggestions and then invite the groups to share their ideas.

If the young people want to take this activity further it could be developed into a larger campaign to keep festivals and music events smoke-free.

# THE GLOBAL PERSPECTIVE

# WHERE IN THE WORLD?

## *Aim*

This sorting activity raises awareness and promotes discussion about the tobacco industry in the developing world.

## *You will need*

- A set of the 'Where in the World?' cards for each group

## *How to do it*

This game introduces young people to the topic of the tobacco industry in low and middle income countries.

It is basically a sorting game; each group is handed a pack of the cards and has to discuss and then agree which information card goes with which country.

Allow about ten minutes for each group to agree their cards and then feed back as a whole group, encouraging discussion and questions. To find out more about the issues raised, encourage the young people to go online to www.ash.org.uk or www.who.int/tobacco.

*Sources:* Brazil, China, Egypt, India – ASH Research Report, *Tobacco: Global Trends* (August 2007); Argentina, Chile, Nigeria, Vietnam – ASH, *You've got to be kidding – how BAT promotes its brands to young people around the world*; Malawi, Rwanda – ASH, *BAT's African Footprint.*

## 'Where in the World' cards

| | | |
|---|---|---|
| **CHINA**<br><br>This country is the largest tobacco-consuming nation in the world. | **INDIA**<br><br>In this country much of the tobacco is consumed in hand-rolled cigarettes known as 'bidis'. | **BRAZIL**<br><br>In this country it would take a tobacco farmer six years to earn what a tobacco company director earns in one day. |
| **EGYPT**<br><br>In this country it is estimated that families spend ten per cent of their household income on tobacco. | **NIGERIA**<br><br>In this country it is still possible to buy single cigarettes (in the UK this was made illegal in 1991). | **MALAWI**<br><br>Tobacco production is a major reason for this country having one of the highest rates of deforestation in the world. |

| | |
|---|---|
| **RWANDA**<br><br>In this country British American Tobacco runs high-profile HIV programmes, branded with its name. | **ARGENTINA**<br><br>In this country BAT advertises its cigarettes on customized websites aimed to attract young people. |
| **VIETNAM**<br><br>In this country cafés are decorated in the colours of cigarette brands and attractive young women are employed to sell cigarettes to customers. | **CHILE**<br><br>Here you can buy cigarettes that open like a book – inside is a phone number that you call to find out the venue for a series of 'secret' parties at summer hot-spots. |

# GLOBAL RESPONSIBILITY

### Aim

This review tool encourages young people to consider the concept of global responsibility and their role within it.

### You will need

- Flipchart paper with the quotes already written on
- Markers
- ASH and WHO information

### How to do it

Divide the young people into small groups seated around tables and hand each table a piece of flipchart paper with one of the quotes on. Give them plenty of markers and invite each group to write comments and responses to the quote on their sheet.

After three minutes call time and collect the papers and then pass them onto the next table, so that each group now has a different opinion to consider, as well as being able to reflect on the previous group's thoughts.

Keep doing this until each group has their original sheet back with them and allow about three minutes for them to see what everyone else has written. Ask each group if any issues or questions have emerged and to share any key points from their sheet.

Finish the activity by asking the group what they think young people can do about this issue. For example, they may want to research it more and take it forward as a campaign issue for their school/youth council. Signpost them to ASH and World Health Organization websites to find out more about the Framework Convention on Tobacco Control and consider developing this into a larger piece of curriculum work.

## GLOBAL RESPONSIBILITY QUOTES

'To suggest that governments in the developing world are not capable of determining their own legislation is insulting and patronizing.' (Suzanne Meldrum, head of corporate communications for British American Tobacco)

'We should recognize that we have a responsibility to people who live outside our own countries, and view ourselves as part of the global community.' (Robyn Richmond, School of Community Medicine, University of New South Wales, Australia)

'I believe that to meet the challenge of our times, human beings will have to develop a greater sense of universal responsibility.' (His Holiness the 14th Dalai Lama)

'Children and women are the prime targets of tobacco companies and have to be protected from being seduced by the tobacco industry. In Pakistan 1200 children take up smoking every day.' (Ali Haider, The Frontier Post, Peshawar, Pakistan)

'There is only one way to reduce the death and suffering caused by the tobacco epidemic, and that is the implementation of effective tobacco control policies.' (World Health Organization, *Tobacco Industry and Corporate Responsibility... An inherent contradiction*)

# WAGES V. PROFITS

## Aim

This creative project aims to raise awareness about the stark differences between the wages of the children employed by the tobacco industry, the cost to the consumer and tobacco company profits.

## You will need

- Empty cigarette cartons contained in a bin bag
- Glue
- Tape
- Markers
- Scissors
- Paper and pens
- Internet access (optional)

## How to do it

To prepare for this activity, collect as many empty cigarette cartons as possible and find out the average cost of a carton in your area. The task is to create a recycled sculpture to represent the 'Tobacco Monster' as a focus for young people to explore how much it costs to smoke and consider how else this money could be spent.

This activity could lead to a much bigger project that looks at the tobacco growers and factory workers, as well as the issue of tax levied on tobacco by governments worldwide. For more information you may want to read *Hard Work, Long Hours, Little Pay* by Plan International (2009), available from www.plan-international.org.

Start the activity by emptying the contents of the bin bag out so that the empty cigarette cartons tumble onto the floor. Explain that on average in the UK a smoker will have paid £7.50 for each packet. Ask for a volunteer to count the packets and then work out how much has been paid in total for the cigarettes. Write this up onto flipchart paper where it can clearly be seen.

Facilitate a discussion that considers:

- How many hours at the minimum wage would they have to work to pay for these?

- Is this money well spent?

Now invite the young people to consider what else the money could be spent on to help developing countries, like Milawi, who are tobacco producers.

Go back to the mound of cigarette packs and set the young people the task of building a sculpture, the 'Tobacco Industry Monster', that raises awareness with other young people about these issues, using the cartons and other craft materials you have prepared. They can use the information you have written on the flipchart to decorate the sculpture or research it further at www.ash.org.uk or by reading *Hard Work, Long Hours, Little Pay*. Hand out paper and pens so that the young people can plan their sculpture before starting work.

Allow time for the young people to build their sculpture, encouraging discussion as they work.

Once the sculpture is complete, display it where other young people can see it and get the message too.

# GETTING THE MESSAGE IN DEVELOPING COUNTRIES

## Aim

This activity raises awareness about some of the marketing strategies employed by tobacco companies in developing countries where the advertising laws are not so strict.

## You will need

- Copies of the 'Policies' sheet
- Flipchart paper and markers

## How to do it

To prepare for the activity, write the information below onto a flipchart sheet and display where everyone in the group can see it.

**FACT FILE**

- Tobacco consumption has fallen over the past 20 years in most high income countries such as Britain, Canada, the United States, Australia and most northern European countries.

- This is not true for other less wealthy parts of the world.

- The World Health Organization predicts that if things don't change there will be 10 million more deaths a year by 2030 and that 70 per cent of these will happen in developing countries such as India, Ghana, Nigeria and Brazil.

Go through the Fact File with the young people and then suggest that one difference between countries where smoking is declining and where it is rising is the advertising regulations. In developing countries the advertising laws are less stringent than in the USA or Europe and marketing tactics directly target children and young people as the potential smokers of tomorrow. For example, in Africa competitions have been held where contestants have to buy cigarettes before being entered into a draw to win a car. Also tobacco companies try to promote a Western image using brand names such as 'Diplomat' (Ghana) and 'High Society' (Nigeria).

In Chile, a tobacco company employs glamorous young women to hand out free cigarettes to children and adults in shopping malls, whilst in Cambodia ice cream wagons have been covered in adverts for cigarettes. Finally, in more than 40 developing countries there is no requirement for health warnings on cigarette packs. If they do appear they are often written in English rather than in local languages.

Divide the young people into groups of four and ask each group to nominate a Youth Minister for Global Tobacco Issues. The rest of the group will be the cabinet, who along with the Minister are set the task of discussing and agreeing a global tobacco marketing and promotion policy to be enforced worldwide. In particular, this needs to reduce the current direct targeting of young people.

Hand each group a flipchart sheet and markers and a copy of the policies. Allow 30 minutes for debate and once decisions have been made bring the whole group back together. Ask each ministry to share their policy, giving the reasons why they have chosen it and why they think it will make a difference.

Finally, hold a vote to decide which ministry made the most effective argument. Allow two votes per person – the group with the most wins! Consider following up this issue by joining the campaign at www.seethroughtheillusion.co.uk to put pressure on the tobacco industry to make positive changes.

*Sources:* ASH Research Report, *Tobacco: Global Trends* (August 2007); ASH, *You've got to be kidding – how BAT promotes its brands to young people around the world*; ASH, *BAT's African Footprint*.

## 'Policies' sheet

### POLICY A

Make it worldwide law that all tobacco products have to contain health warnings that cover at least 30 per cent of the pack.

### POLICY B

Legislate that tobacco companies cannot call their brands anything associated with health, sports or lifestyles.

### POLICY C

Heavily fine any tobacco companies found employing people to promote their products.

### POLICY D

Cancel any events that are sponsored by tobacco companies and ban them from hosting others.

**POLICY E**

Make it illegal to use promotional goods to advertise tobacco products.

**POLICY F**

Ban all competitions that involve tobacco products in any way.

# REVIEW TIPS

# HEALTHY T'S

### Aim

This review activity creates a visual display of anti-smoking messages created by the young people.

### You will need

- String and pegs
- A basic t-shirt shape cut out of flipchart paper for each person
- Magazines
- Scissors and glue

### How to do it

To prepare for the activity, create a card template of a basic t-shirt shape and then draw round it onto flipchart paper (or card) and cut out one for each person taking part.

Open the activity by talking about the way that slogans on t-shirts are used to promote all sorts of things from political messages to rock band tours. Invite the young people to tell you about any t-shirts that they have and why they chose that particular message.

Explain that the task for this activity is to create a t-shirt with an anti-smoking message on it that will appeal to other young people. Hand each person a paper t-shirt and make a good selection of magazines available. They can then look through them to find the letters or words that they want to cut out and use to create their message, and stick it onto the t-shirt.

When everyone has completed their t-shirt, hang up the string to create a washing line and peg the t-shirts onto it.

Leave the washing line on display so that other young people can see the slogans and messages.

# THREE REASONS

### Aim

This is a circle time review activity that reinforces reasons not to smoke, or to quit if you have already started.

### You will need

- Nothing

### How to do it

Sit with the young people in a wide circle. Explain that you are going to ask each person to suggest three reasons either not to smoke, or to give up smoking.

Ideas may include:

- Improve your image – stop your hair, skin and breath smelling of smoke – and make you more appealing to other non-smokers.

- Save money.

- Improve your sense of taste and smell.

- Improve your fitness.

- Boost your confidence.

- Free you from the constant craving for nicotine.

- Become a positive role model for peers, younger siblings and even parents.

Thank each person for their suggestions and summarize the advantages of taking up the idea. Close the circle by offering your own three ideas.

# MOTIVATIONAL WREATH

## *Aim*

This can be done to review learning and create a wreath that displays lots of motivational anti-smoking messages.

## *You will need*

- Multi-coloured paper (cut into large flower shapes)
- A large sheet of stiff white card
- Ribbon
- Glue, scissors, compass and pens

## *How to do it*

To prepare for this activity, make a large circular wreath by cutting out a large doughnut shape of stiff card. The diameter across the centre circle should be at least 30cm, and the width of the doughnut approximately 12cm. Cut a length of ribbon and loop it around and through one side of the doughnut, making sure it is secure as it will be used to hang the wreath when it is complete.

Open the activity by reviewing learning and information gained.

Hand out the paper flowers and distribute the craft equipment. Explain that the task is for each young person to add to the wreath a flower that contains a motivational anti-smoking message, or words of support to those giving up.

When the flowers are complete, carefully glue them close together onto the wreath. There should be no white card visible.

Hang the wreath by the ribbon once all the glue is dry. You now have a motivational wreath to inspire all of the young people in the group.

# ONE-WORD POSTERS

## Aim

This is a review activity that asks young people to share their learning about one aspect of smoking and tobacco products.

## You will need

- Large sheets of cartridge paper
- Markers or paints
- Scrap paper and pencils

## How to do it

Divide the young people into small groups and give each group a word that is related to tobacco or smoking, for example, 'Nicotine', 'Tobacco', 'Cigarette', 'Addiction', 'Quitting'.

Their task is to produce a poster that would appeal to younger children and educate them about what the word means and any dangers associated with it. They can use the scrap paper to agree designs and try out ideas, before transferring the best design onto the thicker paper using marker pens or paint.

Invite each group to present their poster, encouraging questions and debate and leading a round of applause after each turn.

Display the posters so that other young people and children can learn from them.

# ADDITIONAL SUPPORT

### Action on Smoking and Health

www.ash.org.uk

Action on Smoking and Health (ASH) is a campaigning public health charity that works to eliminate the harm caused by tobacco. The website contains information packs, law guides and information about all their current campaigns.

### BBC

www.bbc.co.uk

The BBC website. Put 'smoking and young people' into the site search engine and it takes you to news items, information about youth campaigns and interactive resources about the subject.

### Campaign for Tobacco-Free Kids

www.tobaccofreekids.org

This is an American campaign for 'tobacco-free' children and young people. It has information about the law and health, and reports back on campaigns and also signposts visitors to other sites of interest.

### Cancer Research UK

www.cancerresearchuk.org

Cancer Research UK is the UK's leading charity dedicated to cancer research. The website is packed with information about cancer, including tobacco-related cancers. It also has research to download and a specific news and resources section that includes an area for schools and youth services.

### COST Kids

www.costkids.org/tobacco/tobacco/tobaccoframeset

Children Opposed to Smoking Tobacco is an American anti-tobacco campaign explaining the health dangers of smoking and using chewing tobacco. It also demonstrates how tobacco companies target children.

### Health Canada

www.hc-sc.gc.ca/hc-ps/tobac-tabac/index-eng.php

This Health Canada site has facts about tobacco and Canadian law, as well as health information.

### Oxfam

www.oxfam.orgo.uk

The UK website for Oxfam has information about all their projects and campaigns. Type 'tobacco' into the site search engine and find information about tobacco farming and the global perspective.

### QUIT

www.quit.org.uk

QUIT is an independent UK charity whose aim is to help smokers to stop by offering advice and support. Click through to 'Quit Because Youth Service', which is the section of the site aimed at young people.

### Smoke-Free Movies

www.smokefreemovies.ucsf.edu

Smoke-Free Movies is an American website that campaigns to stop smoking being portrayed in films. It contains facts, pictures and information to support debates around the subject.

### Smokefree

www.smokefree.nhs.uk

NHS website that offers information and support to people trying to stop smoking.

## Tobacco Control

www.tobaccocontrol.bmj.com

Tobacco Control is an international journal covering the nature and consequences of tobacco use worldwide; tobacco's effects on population health, the economy, the environment, and society; efforts to prevent and control the global tobacco epidemic through population level education and policy changes; the ethical dimensions of tobacco control policies; and the activities of the tobacco industry and its allies.